IS-558: Public Works and Disaster Recovery

By

Fema

10/31/2013

Course Overview

This course will explain how public works is involved in disaster recovery. You will learn about planning for recovery and what areas should be considered when planning. You will learn about communicating and coordinating during recovery with others in your agency, with other agencies, and with the public. Because a plan is a "living" document, you'll learn not only how the plan is used during recovery, but how it is updated and maintained during recovery and beyond. You will also learn about mitigation planning and how federal programs can help you achieve your recovery goals.

By the end of this course, you will be able to:

- Explain the role of public works during the recovery period.
- Explain how and why public works should plan for recovery.
- Describe the primary areas that should be included when public works is planning for recovery.
- Describe effective communication and coordination practices during the recovery period.
- Select a course of action based on information in a recovery plan.
- Identify opportunities for achieving recovery goals.

Lesson 1: The Role of Public Works in Recovery

Lesson Overview

When a disaster strikes, public works is not only one of the first responders on the scene, but it is also involved long afterward. Public works professionals are leaders in returning the community to normal, or as near-normal as possible, and they are often the community's most active advocates for mitigation efforts. In this lesson, you will learn about public works' critical role in the recovery process.

Upon completion of this lesson, you should be able to:

- Describe the function of public works in providing key services to the community.
- List recovery activities that are often led or supported by public works.

The Recovery Process

Recovery is an evolving, long-term process that begins soon after the onset of an event and often continues for years. It includes short-term repairs and restoration, as well as long-term permitting, rebuilding, and reconstruction.

Recovery is complex and incorporates consideration of hazard mitigation throughout the process. Successful recovery efforts should include as much of the affected community as is possible.

Whenever practical, normal or routine governmental activity and services need to continue during the recovery process. The recovery of a community is the ultimate responsibility of local officials and community leaders in the public and private sector.

Public Works Functions

Public works provides many key services to a community. These functions may include:

Public Works Functions

Depending on each community's organizational structure, some of these functions may be done by the municipal public works agency, while others may be done by private companies. For the purposes of this course, these activities will be referred to as public works functions, whether they are performed by a public works agency for a municipality, county, tribe, or Native Alaskan village, or by another entity.

Streets and Transportation

Public works agencies are often responsible for the design, construction, and maintenance of:

- Streets
- Bridges
- Sidewalks
- Bike paths
- Stormwater systems

Maintenance may include traffic control, paving and patching, leaf and brush pickup, snow and ice removal, maintaining right-of-way agreements, and other responsibilities.

Sanitation

Sanitation service is a local government service that is possibly the only one that will have an effect on every single resident, and this service often falls under the purview of public works. Sanitation services may also be performed by a governmental agency or a private company.

Sanitation service includes:

- Collection, cleaning, recycling, and disposing of solid waste
- Collection and disposal of household hazardous material

Modern collection processes may include either semi- or fully automated equipment.

Utilities

Public works agencies are often responsible for operating and maintaining watersheds, water filtration plants, and wastewater treatment plants. They may also provide other utility services to the community such as natural gas and electricity, and may be responsible for water, sewer, gas, and power distribution and collection. Utilities may also be provided by governmental agencies or private companies.

Buildings and Grounds

Public works may be responsible for the design, construction, maintenance, and management of public buildings and parks.

Types of Public Buildings:	Types of Grounds:
<ul><li>City halls</li><li>Police stations</li><li>Fire stations</li><li>Community centers</li></ul>	<ul><li>Green spaces</li><li>Parks</li><li>Playgrounds</li><li>Ball fields</li></ul>

<table>
<tr><td>Buildings Services:

• Repair
• Maintenance
• Construction
• Janitorial services</td><td>Grounds Services:

• Tree trimming
• Gardening (plants/ shrubs)
• Mowing
• Other</td></tr>
</table>

Municipal Engineering

The public works agency may be involved in municipal capital projects such as resurfacing, streetlights, facilities, drainage systems, and many other types of projects. This service requires civil and environmental engineering expertise and may include:

- Development, review, and approval
- Facilities and infrastructure design
- Technical studies
- Construction inspection
- Surveying

Fleet Management

Public works agencies are often responsible for procurement and maintenance of city-owned equipment and vehicles. Fleet management may include:

- Equipment and vehicle repairs and maintenance
- New equipment specifications
- Road service
- Fuel management
- Small engine repair
- Other

Management and Administration

Public works agencies may be called upon to provide management and administrative services such as:

- Financial management, reporting, and budgeting
- Public information
- Procurement of professional services
- Requesting and evaluating proposals
- Contract management
- Personnel management
- Operational management
- Data collection and information management

Other Responsibilities

Public works, possibly more than any other municipal function, is a "jack of all trades" and may perform many other responsibilities than what has been listed, such as:

- Cemetery operation and maintenance
- Airport services
- Animal control

Public Works Recovery Activities

Public works has the right and responsibility to get involved in the recovery process. In fact, the public works agency serves a critical function in the recovery process. Public works agencies or their partners construct, manage, and maintain much of the community's critical infrastructure.

During the recovery period, public works plays a vital role in identifying potential mitigation projects to prevent future similar problems, such as widening a culvert to prevent future flooding.

Some of the recovery activities in which public works is often involved include:

- Restoring key services and lifelines
- Rebuilding critical infrastructure
- Continuing damage assessment
- Performing inspections
- Conducting feasibility studies
- Managing debris
- Identifying and initiating mitigation opportunities

Additional information about public works recovery activities can be found in the Manatee County Post Disaster Redevelopment Plan included in the Resources section of the Toolkit. The Toolkit is accessible by clicking on the orange Toolkit icon located at the top of the page.

Lesson Summary

In this lesson, you learned about the role public works plays in disaster recovery. The typical public works functions, such as streets and transportation, sanitation, and municipal engineering, cover a wide array of vital community services making the role of public works in disaster recovery extremely important.

Many recovery activities are often led or supported by public works. These activities include restoring key services, rebuilding critical infrastructure, removing debris, and identifying mitigation opportunities.

The community depends on the public works agency to help return to as near-normal conditions as possible.

Lesson 2: Planning for Recovery

Lesson Overview

Returning to normal (or near-normal) after a disaster doesn't just "happen." Effective recovery is a coordinated effort among local government agencies, citizens, the private sector, voluntary organizations, neighboring jurisdictions, and the state and federal government.

The recovery process requires planning by more than just the local emergency management agency. For all parties to work together seamlessly after a disaster, plans and agreements must be put into place well in advance, and all parties involved in recovery should also be involved in planning. In this lesson, you will learn about how and why public works should plan for recovery.

Upon completion of this lesson, you will be able to:

- Explain the importance of planning for recovery.
- Identify key stakeholders and partners who can contribute to the public works recovery plan.
- Describe administrative considerations for public works recovery planning.
- Describe the information needed to create the recovery plan.
- List avenues for acquiring additional resources to assist with recovery needs.
- Explain how risk and vulnerability assessment information is used for recovery planning.

The Importance of Planning for Recovery

Public works emergency management planning for the recovery process is an integral part of the overall community-wide planning process for managing a disaster.

Planning for recovery is important because it:

- Helps establish the mission
- Considers community-specific events
- Helps guide the recovery effort
- Sets the stage for identifying potential mitigation opportunities
- Integrates public works recovery activity with other agencies
- Helps identify stakeholders and partners
- Reduces possible future losses
- Helps achieve community consensus
- Integrates public works knowledge and unique funding opportunities into the overall planning process
- Is required for some federal funding

Voices of Experience: The Importance of Planning for Recovery

These public works experts were asked to share their thoughts on the importance of planning for recovery.

Kenneth Miller - Director of Public Works (retired), Village of Mundelein, IL:

Being prepared for a long-term emergency and recovery operation should be done at the same time, right from the beginning. It's important to do that so that you have efficiency and fluency as you move from the response to the recovery operation mode of your event.

You need to document everything. FEMA, insurance companies, even the constituents within your own community, will want to know what was done, when it was done, and how much did it cost to do it.

Try to establish formalized mutual aid agreements and other agreements for other resources that might be needed in an event- especially events that may be more prone to your area, such as near rivers.

Documented agreements are the only way to be reimbursed by either the insurance or FEMA. So it is vitally important to put somebody on documentation from the start, right through the finish.

Review what went right, what went wrong, and be honest about it. Make the changes you can and understand that there are some things that you truly cannot plan or work around.

Most of all, I would say, understand and keep reminding yourself and others as you need to that this too will pass, just like every other bad day. All you can do is focus on making tomorrow better from the lessons you've learned today and yesterday.

Gregg Varner - Director of Solid Waste (retired), County of Charleston, SC:

In 1989, Hurricane Hugo came across the state of South Carolina. Those of us in the local jurisdictions—I was with the City of North Charleston—we spent a good bit of time working with the County of Charleston for managing debris. And we were all a little bit unskilled, you might say. We hadn't had a whole lot of training, but we did get our hands on debris management guides and work through that kind of thing.

The importance of thinking about it from a recovery perspective is when Hurricane Hugo came through, after the cleanup effort was completed, an awful lot of building materials and some tree debris went in the landfill. What we discovered, when it was all said and done, is that the Charleston County Landfill had actually used up 20 years of landfill life as a result of that hurricane coming through.

So, in thinking about recovery, knowing that for us in public works, debris management is a major recovery issue, you've got to ask yourself, "What's the life of my landfill?" Because one hurricane like Hurricane Hugo, taking 20 years, could eat up your landfill life. So, where do you go from there?

John Pennington - Director, Department of Emergency Management, Snohomish County, WA:

One thing for public works entities to remember is that planning is actually becoming a required element of emergency management in order to receive future federal funding.

A good example of this is the Disaster Mitigation Act of 2000 which required that emergency management departments or jurisdictions develop certain plans before they could receive federal funds after a disaster event. And, slowly but surely, it appears that the federal government is moving the direction by which public works, emergency management, and other critical departments in local state governments are going to be required to continue planning and enhance their planning to be able to receive future federal funds including recovery planning.

Kurt Blomquist - Public Works Director, City of Keene, NH:

In 2005, the city of Keene, we had flooding in our downtown area. Over forty percent of our areas were under four to six feet of water. One of the things we learned in that process was as soon as we started the response, people started asking the questions about what are we going to do with our stuff, our damaged goods? We started talking about, well, what are we going to do with materials that are left beside the road? How are we going to help our residents in beginning the cleaning up? And that process began literally within hours of the EOC activating.

Since that point, we sat down as a department and developed recovery plans, because we've recognized that we need to know, and people need to know, what's going to happen. Whether it's removal of organic debris, trees, limbs, those kind of materials, or if it's going to be materials from houses—grandma's sofa—anything that folks had in the basement.

For at least us in public works, it is a huge, huge operation, and having the right people, at the time that these efforts start, is critical. We've had to identify contractors that have certain capabilities and we have communications with them now that if we get into a situation, they would be available. We've worked with our local hauling company to make sure that they would be available and be willing to support us first in providing packers and other things like that.

This really came home recently with Hurricane Irene. We were very fortunate that we were not hit significantly. But, we had activated our actual recovery and our clean-up plans even before the hurricane hit the area.

Establishing the Planning Team

The public works agency should identify and invite stakeholders and partners to the planning process for recovery. The planning team should include public works agency supervisors or functional directors representing roads and bridges, utilities, facilities, sanitation, parks, fleet management, and other public works functions.

Additional stakeholders and partners may include:

- Emergency management representatives or liaisons
- Other local public works agencies
- Private utilities and engineers
- Department of Health, as a regulatory agency
- Corresponding state agencies
- Historic preservation officers and environmental liaisons
- Financial and procurement representatives

Administrative Considerations

During the planning process, decisions are required in order to assign roles and responsibilities within the public works function. These decisions will help provide a necessary framework to accomplish the administrative duties needed in recovering from a disaster, such as the considerations shown on the graphics.

Staffing Considerations

A planning coordinator should be identified who will be responsible for assigning roles and responsibilities associated with planning. Other tasks associated with staffing considerations may include:

- Preparing the plan
- Reviewing and approving the plan
- Identifying staffing needs
- Identifying training needs
- Coordinating with state and federal agencies
- Initiating mutual aid agreements and contracts
- Coordinating with emergency management and other agencies
- Determining appropriate use and management of volunteers

Legal Considerations

There are always legal considerations with respect to emergency management. All local professionals, including the public works professional, should seek legal advice in the development of plans, procedures, authorities, and policies.

Tasks associated with legal considerations may include:

- Reviewing ordinances that address and reflect recovery or other emergency management issues, such as building codes
- Reviewing contracts and agreements, such as waste disposal contracts

- Monitoring equity of administrative aspects, such as emergency procurement codes
- Assisting with document preparation, such as interagency agreements
- Considering litigation and claims
- Documenting an equitable and competitive procurement process

Keep in mind that emergency procurement codes may allow you to purchase items differently in an emergency than under normal circumstances. Proposal periods are likely to be shortened and credit limits may be raised. You should research procurement codes in your area so you understand them well *before* a disaster strikes.

Financial Considerations

The local community must consider whether it is able to finance the disaster recovery process. The financial team for the local government should evaluate possible funding mechanisms to support local efforts until federal funds are made available as well as to supplement federal funds. Personnel should be assigned to coordinate financial issues that may arise due to a disaster or other emergency.

Tasks associated with financial considerations may include:

- Estimating the cost of recovery activity and available local funding
- Understanding potential reimbursable actions in federal programs such as the Stafford Act
- Researching existing practices regarding cost-sharing arrangements with state and federal agencies, and pre-establishing cost-sharing arrangements as needed
- Considering impact to local tax and revenue structure
- Exploring other potential sources of revenue
- Monitoring equitable emergency procurement

Documentation Considerations

Proper documentation is vital to effective emergency management. An important part of establishing documentation procedures is pre-identifying the agencies and individuals who will be responsible for documentation during a local event.

Consider the need for documentation related to accountability, planning, and finances such as the following:

- Adherence to state and federal requirements
- Project worksheets
- Progress reports
- Contracts for goods or services
- Expenditures for recovery activity
- All other agreements
- Lessons learned
- Potential litigation and audit

- Electronic records and files

When you have documented everything, be sure to make multiple copies and keep files for your records. It is also best to have a backup of the files in a separate location.

Information Gathered by a Planning Team

In order to plan effectively for disaster recovery, the planning team needs to gather a great deal of information so priorities can be established, responsibilities can be assigned, and equipment and resources can be allocated appropriately.

Information to be gathered during the planning process includes:

- Pre-event priorities
- Community demographics
- Availability of resources (in-house/other)
- Inventory and availability of goods and supplies
- Jurisdictional responsibilities
- Community-wide recovery plan
- Risk and vulnerability assessments
- Pre-established contracts

Planning for Resource Needs

At the onset of a major event, the public works agency, as well as others, will likely be beyond their means. Managers will need to exercise a high level of creativity to plan for adequate resources based on the newly established priorities.

Efforts should be made to utilize local resources as much as possible. When additional resources are needed, they may be acquired through:

- Redirected existing in-house resources
- Mutual aid/ Memoranda of Understanding (MOUs)
- Contracting for private resources
- State and federal agencies

Following a large scale event, the public works agency will need to procure or initiate high-dollar contracts for purchasing goods. Planning for a legally defensible emergency procurement process is a necessity. Establishing agreements, contracts, and emergency procurement procedures prior to an event whenever feasible will facilitate a more accountable and effective response and recovery period after an event.

Using Hazard Analysis Information to Plan for Recovery

Risk and vulnerability assessment information drives the planning process as it relates to identifying the needed information to be gathered by the planning team. Every community is different, so it is critical that you identify hazards that are most likely to affect you.

Remember, risk assessments provide information about what hazards are likely to occur in your community by answering the question, "What could happen to adversely impact the community?"

Vulnerability assessments include information about how often each hazard is likely to occur, the area likely to be impacted, and how severe the impact may be. This assessment answers the question, "How and where could each hazard affect the community?"

Although every community is different, there are some basic steps that need to be performed to effectively assess risks and vulnerabilities for the community. These common steps are shown on the graphic collectively as the Hazard Analysis Process.

Critical Infrastructure and Key Resources

Both risk and vulnerability assessments identify the impact of an event on the public works critical infrastructure and key resources (CIKR) in your community.

As you may recall from previous courses, critical infrastructure and key resources are the components that are necessary for the health and welfare of the population of your community. These components include public safety services, health care, utilities, transportation systems, and lifelines.

In addition, critical infrastructure and key resources include facilities that, if impacted by a hazard event, could result in high potential loss or release of hazardous materials, which would further result in significant environmental impacts if not addressed by public works or others in the response process.

Lesson Summary

In this lesson, you learned that planning for recovery is crucial for your community and your public works agency. Successful planning allows priorities to be established, responsibilities to be assigned, and equipment and resources to be allocated.

Remember, key stakeholders should be involved in the planning process for recovery. A coordinated effort in emergency management planning will help your community return to normal (or near-normal) following a disaster.

Keep in mind that there are several administrative factors the planning team will need to consider, and that it's important to plan for the use of additional resources if recovery needs overwhelm the community.

To determine potential recovery needs, the planning team will need to review a great deal of information. In particular, risk and vulnerability assessments provide valuable information for the team.

Lesson 3: Recovery Plan Components

Lesson Overview

In this lesson, you will learn about the primary areas that should be included when public works is planning for recovery.

Upon completion of this lesson, you will be able to:

- Identify critical infrastructure and key resources for which public works may have responsibility during recovery.
- Describe how the public works agency may be involved in protecting public safety and health during the recovery period.
- List environmental concerns for which public works may provide support during the recovery period.
- Describe how inspection services contribute to the recovery process.
- List support services that public works may provide to other agencies during the recovery period.
- Describe components of a debris management plan that should be considered during recovery.

Planning for Recovery Priorities

Priorities within a community should be established prior to an event or disaster as much as is practical.

Consideration should be given to all critical infrastructure and key resources (CIKR) identified in the most recent version of the local Natural Hazard Mitigation Plan (NHMP), which is required to be updated every five years, or the Hazard Inventory and Vulnerability Analysis (HIVA). Public works CIKR may include roads, bridges, utilities, and other assets.

In addition to establishing the public works recovery planning team, many communities will establish a community-wide Recovery Task Force (RTF) or Long Term Recovery Committee (LTRC). These task forces may include several representatives from within the Emergency Operations Center (EOC), as well as community stakeholders and partners similar to those identified in the public works planning team. The RTF or LTRC will participate in the development and implementation of the community-wide redevelopment plan. You will learn more about these task forces later in this course.

Recovery Priorities

Restoration or short-term recovery priorities are based upon:

- Critical needs, such as safety and preservation of life

- Economic needs and support to the local business community
- Community needs or expected basic services for neighborhoods or subdivisions

Remember, efforts should be made to utilize local resources; however, it is likely that mutual aid or contracting will be required to restore critical services in a timely manner. Attempts should be made to pre-establish such agreements prior to an event or disaster.

Recovery Priorities: Conducting Damage Assessment

Immediately following an event or a disaster, one of the most significant challenges for the public works agency is detection and isolation of damages to critical infrastructure and facilities. This activity begins during the response effort and is likely to continue during the recovery period.

When planning for damage assessment, the public works agency should consider:

- Public works critical facilities and key resources, as identified in the NHMP and HIVA/hazard analysis
- Roles and responsibilities of the public works agency
- Priorities established in the planning process
- Definition of the processes and standards that will be used for assessment, documentation, and reporting (must be comprehensive and legally defensible)
- Establishment of first in teams (as an option)
- Detailed information needed and the flow of that information
- Importance of accuracy

Why Plan for Damage Assessment?

Planning for damage assessment will help to ensure that the process goes smoothly when a disaster strikes. It will also assist in "institutionalizing" the process of damage assessment for future public works professionals. Without prior planning, damage detection may be inadequate, resulting in:

- Slow or delayed response and recovery effort
- The possibility of a delayed or denied Presidential Disaster Declaration
- Inaccurate portrayal of new priorities
- Inaccurate or ill-informed decision making by senior elected officials or policy makers
- Potential for cascading impacts from damages or destruction
- Discovery of "hidden damages" after the potential for reimbursement has closed
- Significant environmental impact
- Issues of public safety or health

Isolation of damages allows for the conservation of valuable resources. In addition, it will provide for more timely restoration and reconstruction.

Recovery Priorities: Providing Essential Services

Following a disaster or other emergency, the public works agency should continue to provide day-to-day services as much as possible, and this requires prior planning. Diligent efforts should be made to return the community to normal; it will aid the community-wide recovery effort and possibly prevent a disaster within a disaster.

To ignore certain day-to-day operations, such as sanitation or household garbage collection and disposal, may create additional and unnecessary issues that require involvement of other government agencies (e.g., Public Health) and can inadvertently slow the overarching community recovery effort.

The restoration of regular local government services is a key aspect of the public works recovery effort. Damaged lifelines such as utilities, roads and bridges, or public facilities should be identified and prioritized during the damage assessment process.

Recovery Priorities: Restoring Critical Infrastructure and Key Resources

Critical infrastructure and key resources (CIKR) should be identified in the vulnerability assessment process. Consideration of the impact of community exposures or hazards will help set pre-event priorities for restoration or reconstruction.

After a disaster, with current event damage assessment in hand, "new" priorities for repair and reconstruction of critical infrastructure and key resources are possible during the recovery period.

Critical infrastructure and key resources for which public works may be responsible include:

- Highways, roads, and bridges (transportation systems)
- Surface water systems
- Water and wastewater treatment, distribution, and collection
- Public transit, railroads, and airports
- Communications facilities
- Public buildings and facilities
- Solid waste facilities

Recovery Priorities: Protecting Public Safety and Health

Protection of life is the top priority for all local governmental agencies, including the public works agency, as first responders. There are several public safety or public health issues for which the public works agency will provide support, including:

- Emergency power

* Enforcement of curfews
* Re-entry procedures
* Hazardous materials incidents
* Traffic control and management
* Animal and vector control
* Food distribution sites
* Mortuary facilities
* Secondary threats or hazards

Recovery Priorities: Protecting the Environment

There may be environmental concerns that exist which require public works to act as the lead agency or, at a minimum, a responsible entity for providing support. Potential issues in which public works may be involved include:

* Addressing contamination of surface water or drinking water
* Clearing and cleaning canals and other storm drainage systems
* Disposal of household garbage or household hazardous materials
* Debris management
* Addressing air quality issues
* Re-vegetation
* Coastal management, such as beach re-nourishment
* Wetlands revitalization
* Historic preservation

Recovery Priorities: Performing Inspection Services

Inspection services involve the determination of whether repair or reconstruction is allowed for damaged building or facilities. They may also support the community-wide effort, providing assistance to other agencies and supporting all emergency management activity. During recovery, inspection services may provide technical support to other agencies.

The basic issues or functions of inspection services may include:

* Damage assessment
* Inspection priorities
* In-house vs. contracting for services
* Use of outside resources such as Hazards U.S. Multi-Hazard (HAZUS-MH) or similar programs
* Issuance of building permits
* Post disaster permitting procedures
* Determination of habitability
* Policy or procedure development
* Local management of contractors
* Code or ordinance review and update

- Training and exercise participation

Inspection Services

Inspection services may examine damages to homes, businesses, industry, or other private structures. These services may include:

- Establishment of inspection request procedures
- Inspections for life safety and structural integrity, code compliance, and reconstruction or rebuilding activity
- Establishment of a building tagging system

Inspection services should ensure that the public is informed of their procedures for inspection, permitting, and technical assistance. They should work within the established Public Information system in place for the local government.

Inspection services should also secure documentation of all activity as called for in the community's established documentation process.

Recovery Priorities: Providing Support Services

In addition to the recovery efforts previously described, the public works agency will provide support to other local agencies. Possible support services activity may include:

- Technical and engineering services
- Community wide damage assessment
- Temporary repairs
- Provide cost estimates
- Status updates
- Input for ordinance or code review
- Assist with public information
- Support the community wide emergency management of the event or disaster
- Coordination with state or federal agencies
- Evaluation of lessons learned

Recovery Priorities: Managing Debris

It is likely that debris as a result of a disaster-related event will have an immediate and universal impact on all citizens in the affected area. Debris management is the responsibility of local government and, in most cases, is assigned to the public works agency, engineering staff, or the solid waste/environmental services function.

Coordination with federal, state, and local officials, including tribal officials or Native Alaskan villages, is a necessity and is always beneficial to development and implementation of debris management plans. This function requires the deployment of a significant volume of resources and is often a very expensive operation.

Different types of debris, as shown below, require different methods of disposal, so it is important to have a plan in place for handling each type.

Debris Management Plan

Public works officials should develop a comprehensive debris management plan *prior* to an event or disaster. Resources are available to prepare such a plan and often include the assistance of the Federal Emergency Management Agency (FEMA) as well as state emergency management agencies.

Having a FEMA-approved Debris Management Plan has significant benefits for a community. Approved plans are viewed by FEMA as a pre-existing standard operating policy that allows for quicker review and allocation of federal reimbursement costs for debris management. Additionally, recent federal policies (currently under review) have recognized the value of such pre-approved plans by allowing for a greater percentage of federal cost-share and retention of salvage value of recyclable debris during the recovery process.

Is It Reimbursable?

Although removal of debris from private property is generally not considered a reimbursable expense under the Public Assistance (PA) program, there are certain situations where removal may be allowed.

Some examples include:

- Debris that is blocking a primary ingress or egress route
- Debris that has become or may become a public health hazard
- Debris that substantially threatens additional damage to improved property, public ingress or egress, or public rights of way
- Household hazardous waste debris

When developing your debris management plan, seek consultation regarding the acceptable financial risk your jurisdiction is willing to accept regarding removal of debris from private property.

Components of a Debris Management Plan

Key components of the debris management plan include:

- Right-of-way clearance and removal
- Private property removal
- Establishing priorities

- Public vs. private roads
- Debris reduction facilities or plans
- Recycling efforts
- Hazardous materials
- Household hazardous materials
- Cost of collection and disposal
- Disposal facilities, landfill capacity
- Temporary site management
- Contracting for services
- Contract monitoring
- Appropriate separation of debris from multiple disaster events

When two events occur within a short span and your jurisdiction has two Stafford Act declarations, you need to separate the debris if possible. For example, if your community was affected by a snow event that was followed a few weeks later by a flood event, you will have two types of debris: collapsed roofs from the snow, and flood debris. These need to be separated or FEMA may disqualify some expenses from being reimbursable because they were submitted under the wrong disaster declaration.

Debris Management Resources

Several resources to assist you with debris management have been provided in the Toolkit for this course, accessible by selecting the icon at the top of the screen.

You can learn more about debris management by taking G202, Debris Management or IS-632.a, Introduction to Debris Operations. Your State Training Officer should be able to provide information about upcoming offerings of G202. You can access the IS-632.a course at EMI's training website. In addition, FEMA has developed a guide to help you develop a debris management plan, FEMA 325 Debris Management Guide.

Links to the EMI's website, the FEMA Debris Management Guide, and a sample debris management plan are included in the Resources section of the Toolkit. You can use the sample plan as an example to jumpstart the development of your own unique plan.

Lesson Summary

In this lesson, you learned that after a disaster, the top priority for any first responder, including public works, is protecting public safety and health.

You learned how public works is involved in protecting and restoring the environment, restoring services, repairing or rebuilding critical infrastructure and key resources, performing inspection services, and providing support services that are important to an effective recovery.

You also learned about the components of a debris management plan that should be considered during the recovery period and were provided with some resources for learning more about debris management and developing a plan.

Lesson 4: Communication and Coordination

Lesson Overview

After a disaster, many different individuals, agencies, and organizations, (and often multiple jurisdictions) must work together to be able to restore the affected areas to as near pre-disaster condition as possible. Coordination and communication are vital to successful emergency management, beginning with planning efforts and continuing through recovery actions.

In this lesson, you will learn about effective communication and coordination practices during the recovery period.

Upon completion of this lesson, you will be able to:

- List methods for coordinating the recovery efforts of the public works agency with those of the community.
- Describe the information that should be communicated with other agencies during recovery.
- Describe the information that should be communicated to the public during recovery.
- Explain how to involve the public in the recovery process.

Coordinating Recovery Efforts

The public works agency is a critical participant in the coordination of local emergency management activity and, in particular, recovery efforts.

Public works officials must coordinate the public works recovery effort with the community-wide recovery effort, including planning efforts as well as implementation of the recovery plan after a disaster. It is prudent to assign the coordination responsibility to one or more persons within the public works agency. Since some projects may require public and private financial support, public-private partnerships should be considered for the coordination of those projects.

The recovery plan should be coordinated with other local plans from several sources, such as the following:

Public Works

Public works' local recovery plans can include:

- Floodplain Management Plan
- Stormwater Management Plan
- Debris Management Plan
- Capital Improvements Plan
- Subdivision Ordinances

- Land Development Code
- Building Codes

Emergency Management

Emergency management's local recovery plans may be "stand alone" plans or may be a consortium of plans that include:

- Comprehensive Emergency Management Plan (CEMP) or Emergency Operations Plan (EOP)
- Continuity of Operations Plan (COOP)
- Continuity of Government Plan (COG)
- Local or Regional Evacuation Plan
- Natural Hazard Mitigation Plan (NHMP)
- Flood Response Plan
- Temporary Disaster Housing Plan
- National Flood Insurance Program (NFIP)
- NFIP Community Rating System
- Functional Needs Populations Plan

Financing Authority

Local recovery plans need to be coordinated with the plans of the local government budget agency or department because of the financial support required for the recovery efforts in your community.

Other

Other local recovery plans can include:

- Open Space Management Plan
- Natural Resource Protection Plan
- Comprehensive Land Use Plan
- Economic Development Plan
- Historic Preservation Plan
- Zoning Ordinances
- Fire Code

Methods for Coordinating Recovery

To effectively coordinate recovery efforts of the public works agency with those of the community, consider using the following methods:

- Assign dedicated personnel and/or liaisons to the recovery function.
- Ensure that public works is "subscribed" to all recovery function email lists.

- Proactively reach out via phone and email to critical recovery partners. Introduce yourself as the liaison for public works.
- Personally inquire and attend all recovery-like meetings, even at times when public works is not normally included. Do not be afraid to insert yourself and public works into the process.
- Ensure that existing Memoranda of Understanding (MOUs) and mutual aid agreements that involve public works are recognized and adhered to.

The Importance of Communication

Communication following an event or disaster is important to the recovery effort. Depending on the nature of the event, communication and public information related to the event will potentially need to continue for months or years. The communications mission is to deliver accurate information in a timely manner, with an emphasis on saving or protecting lives and property.

The community should utilize all communication strategies as defined by the National Incident Management System (NIMS). As you may recall, these strategies were reviewed in the IS-552 course, *The Public Works Role in Emergency Management*.

National Incident Management System (NIMS)

The National Incident Management System (NIMS) provides a systematic, proactive approach to guide departments and agencies at all levels of government, nongovernmental organizations, and the private sector to work seamlessly to prevent, protect against, respond to, recover from, and mitigate the effects of incidents, regardless of cause, size, location, or complexity, in order to reduce the loss of life and property and harm to the environment.

NIMS works hand in hand with the National Response Framework (NRF). NIMS provides the template for the management of incidents, while the NRF provides the structure and mechanisms for national-level policy for incident management.

Additional information about NIMS communication strategies is available on the Resources page included in the Toolkit.

Communication During Recovery

Communication, as it relates to the community and the public works agency in recovery, is far reaching. In many cases, public works may very well be the lead agency in recovery efforts such as utility restoration or debris management. In one way or another, public works is a player in nearly all aspects of recovery.

As a result, communication of issues such as the recovery work itself, schedules, timelines, warnings, etc. are critical. The lack of this type of communication is likely to delay the recovery effort and frustrate other agencies and the public.

Public works, in cooperation with the Public Information Officer (PIO), must keep local, state, and federal agencies, as well as the public, informed regarding all agency recovery efforts, including debris management, rebuilding of infrastructure, implementation of mitigation projects, and other actions.

Intra-Agency Communication

Communications with other agencies such as other local public works entities, state or federal liaisons should, at a minimum, include:

- Updates to current disaster information
- Updates to damage assessment
- Strategies or plans for recovery
- Specific resource needs
- Financial impacts
- Environmental concerns
- Changes to service levels

During recovery, public works' information is often the most important information an emergency manager (EM) or Public Information Officer (PIO) can receive. Public works should not wait to be asked for an update. The public works official should automatically update the PIO or EM when there is information that needs to be pushed out.

Communication with the Public

Throughout the recovery process, the public should continue to be informed regarding activities or plans for the community. Information that should be conveyed to the public during recovery includes warnings or potential life safety issues the public may face. Recovery plans that exist within the community should also be shared.

The public should also be informed about how the community has been or is expected to be impacted due to changes in services or infrastructure reconstruction during recovery. The public should also be aware of where and how to gather additional information about the recovery process and programs such as Individual Assistance. Some of the outlets for dissemination of information include news releases, Public Service Announcements (PSA), and social media.

During some recovery efforts, it is critical to have a public works liaison appointed to the ESF-15 Public Information Function in order to ensure that the public is informed.

Public Involvement in Recovery

The planning process and valid plans should incorporate community input. As a result, there will more likely be an inclusive plan with community support; yielding positive results.

Keep in mind that public communication should not only be one-way. Consider holding town hall meetings and conducting surveys to get the public's input on recovery and mitigation projects, including utilization of online forums and social media. Be sure to communicate instructions for community participation in these recovery activities, and why these activities are important to the process.

Public involvement can reach beyond traditional jurisdictional boundaries to include regional collaboration as well. Remember, effective communication and coordination go hand-in-hand. Your public information efforts must be coordinated with other agencies, organizations, and jurisdictions involved, to ensure that a clear, consistent message is conveyed.

Lesson Summary

In this lesson, you learned how to coordinate the public works recovery effort with the community-wide recovery effort. Effective coordination requires effective communication, both with other agencies involved and with the public. This can be accomplished by providing accurate information in a timely manner.

Remember, public involvement in the recovery process generates buy-in and leads to success.

Lesson 5: Recovery Implementation and Maintenance

Lesson Overview

After a disaster, there will likely be many competing priorities on the way to restoring the community to as near-normal as possible. It is important for your public works agency and the community as a whole to be able to choose the recovery actions that will best help meet the community's and agency's recovery goals while working within budget, time, and other constraints that exist. You will also need to update the recovery plan when priorities change or new information becomes available.

In this lesson, you will learn to select a course of action based on information in a recovery plan. Upon completion of this lesson, you will be able to:

- Describe the function of the Recovery Task Force or Long Term Recovery Committee.
- List recommended steps for recovering after a disaster.
- Explain how the recovery plan is used, updated, and maintained throughout the recovery period.
- Determine recovery priorities based on disaster information.
- Choose a feasible, sustainable recovery project that meets the community's and agency's recovery goal for a given scenario.

Implementing the Recovery Plan

Without a follow-through process, the recovery plan is little more than a report. Implementation is the key to community recovery. In the case of public works, if projects related to essential services and critical infrastructure are not completed, the recovery process is halted.

The necessary political or policy approval from the governing body should be acquired for the public works recovery effort as well as for the community-wide plan.

As you may recall, public-private partnerships should be considered for coordinating the implementation of recovery projects.

Establishing the Recovery Task Force

A Recovery Task Force (RTF) or Long Term Recovery Committee (LTRC) should be established to help develop the community-wide redevelopment plan, coordinate efforts, and address unmet needs in the community in addition to other functions. Some communities may have different terms for a recovery function but they will often have many similarities. Whereas most Emergency Operations Centers (EOC) are coordinated or led by emergency management professionals and staffed with first responders, recovery entities are often **coordinated by**

emergency management and staffed with policy experts. These experts are usually critical partners or agencies and often include the legislative or executive branch of a jurisdiction.

Task Force Functions

The task force or committee will also participate in the development of policies and procedures for redevelopment, including potential streamlining of otherwise cumbersome processes (e.g., permit issuance). This may require code or ordinance changes that allow for the establishment of and authorities for an RTF or LTRC.

The RTF or LTRC will also identify possible mitigation opportunities and assist with reviewing current event/disaster status. Based on these findings, the team will offer recommendations for local laws, ordinances, and zoning, and make suggestions for new operational protocols or standard operating procedures (SOPs). For example, the task force may recommend changing ordinances regarding positioning of billboards to protect nearby properties from high wind damages, or they may recommend relocating a highway out of a flood zone.

The task force or committee can also identify potential sources of existing or new funding opportunities and solicit a consensus for the community-wide recovery plan.

Coordinating Recovery Efforts

When recovering after a disaster, public works should consider the following steps:

The first step in the disaster recovery planning process is to assess the damages that have occurred as a result of the specific event.

The second step is to prioritize the issues that are affecting your jurisdiction. By prioritizing these issues your community can determine its course of action.

Once a course of action has been determined, it is necessary to obtain authority to act upon those priorities.

The next step is to initiate the project and coordinate with the appropriate partners in order to address the priorities.

Finally, review your progress and adjust accordingly. Throughout the recovery process, developing situations and new information will bring about the need to reevaluate priorities. Monitoring progress and maintaining flexibility will help lead to a more successful recovery process.

By coordinating a process that works with the community-wide recovery effort, public works will be better able to help the community recover from a hazard event and return to normal, or to as near pre-event condition as possible.

Updating the Recovery Plan

The recovery plan should be considered a tool to guide both the community-wide and public works recovery processes. It requires action and accomplishment, but can change as the process moves forward. Once completed, the plan will undergo public scrutiny. That will continue as the recovery proceeds. Continued policy changes and approvals may be necessary as the process evolves.

During the implementation of the recovery plan, projects will be planned, designed, funded, approved, and completed. The needed resources and funding must be reevaluated project-by-project. As the plan evolves and projects are completed, the plan is revised.

Development and implementation of a public works recovery plan establishes the basic footprint of the public works recovery process. This process may take years to complete, is contingent upon available funding, and is designed based on the extent and nature of the damage and continued public scrutiny.

Building and Maintaining Community Support for Recovery

Solicitation of community support from citizens and stakeholders continues throughout the recovery period. Stakeholders and citizens must be made to feel they are a part of the implementation and update processes. Consider posting the recovery framework online so that non-sensitive information is available to the public. In this way, the public has a greater understanding of the road to recovery and progress toward recovery goals is more visible.

The recovery process must be monitored closely. It is important that results are visible as soon as is possible. Reports and public presentations should be made available throughout the recovery period. Otherwise, community support may break down, having a negative effect on the recovery process as a whole.

Maintaining the Recovery Plan

Maintaining the recovery plan should also include a review of the basic components including administration planning, plan development, and implementation. Remember to address key issues such as resource management, communication, and public information.

Documentation of project implementation is essential to a successful recovery and the development of lessons learned or an after-action report. It is also necessary to ensure accountability of the expenditure of public funds.

In that the recovery process is often accomplished in years rather than months, there are other considerations to maintaining an active and continuing recovery plan. Some examples are:

- New priorities
- Policies or procedures

- Analysis criteria
- Process or plan development
- Training and exercises
- Roles and responsibilities
- Funding availability

Determining Recovery Priorities

When establishing recovery priorities to include in the plan, consider the general prioritization of:

- Critical Infrastructure and Key Resources
- Economic Impacts
- Community Needs
- Public Health Concerns

Also consider the pre-event public works priorities, as established in the risk and vulnerability assessments. Keep in mind that damage assessment information may identify new priorities. Additionally, consider planning criteria specifically related to public works agency recovery activities such as utility restoration, garbage collection, and water/sewage treatment.

Critical Infrastructure and Key Resources (CIKR)

Remember, critical infrastructure and key resources are the components that are necessary for the health and welfare of the population of your community. Many CIKR fall under the scope of public works, which may have the lead on many of these projects. Restoration of essential services and repair, as well as rebuilding of key assets are high priorities for any community's recovery (e.g., reconstructing a bridge).

Economic Impacts

Each hazard can have a different economic impact on a community. For example, when a storm disrupts power in a commercial district, restoring that power is essential for the economic recovery of those businesses and the community as well.

Community Needs

When creating the recovery plan, consider the number of households who could be displaced by a disaster, the number of individuals who may need public shelters, and the need for social services such as counseling or financial assistance. Public works should be aware that they may be called upon to support things such as public shelters with the installation of generators or locating port-a-lets. Keep in mind that plans for recovery actions may change when actual information about community needs is available after a disaster, causing a need for your plan to be updated.

Public Health Concerns

Public health concerns are also an important consideration for public works and other agencies during recovery. The recovery plan should cover keeping essential services operational. For example, the interruption of services such as routine household solid waste collection, a wastewater treatment facility, or a water treatment plant, could all have negative effects on the public health.

By planning for these public health concerns, your community will be better able to recover.

Identifying Potential Recovery Projects

Projects should be broken down by both short- and long-term recovery objectives.

Short-Term Recovery Projects

Short-term recovery projects are generally those that allow citizens to re-inhabit their homes and neighborhoods. Examples include:

- Opening roads and highways
- Restoring utilities
- Assessing damage
- Supporting other agencies
- Evaluating resource needs
- Initiating contracts for services

Long-Term Recovery Projects

Long-term recovery projects often involve activities and actions taken to return a community to pre-disaster condition, or as near pre-disaster condition as possible. Examples include:

- Policy and/or ordinance changes
- Removal and disposal of disaster debris
- Repair and restoration of critical infrastructure/facilities
- Inspection services
- Hazard mitigation planning
- Historical preservation

Selecting Recovery Projects to Implement

Identification of recovery projects will generally result in a comprehensive list, and it is unlikely that there will be enough funding for all identified recovery projects. The resulting competition for funding, therefore, must be addressed and structured professionally in order to ensure a unified recovery effort.

Selection should be based on priorities set with criteria to include life safety issues; restoration of those services critical to the community; and reconstruction of critical infrastructure, the local economy, and the community's quality of life.

Ultimately, the evaluation process must consider:

- Newly established priorities
- The mission of the public works agency and public works services
- Overall community recovery effort or defined goals
- Cost and available financial resources

Implementation Criteria

A review system or criteria should be established to rate or review each potential project. The system should have a focus on the needs of the community, the project feasibility, and sustainability.

Issues should be considered such as:

- Quality of life
- Economic impact
- Social equity
- Environmental concerns
- Hazard mitigation value
- Community support
- Relation to other projects
- Time to complete
- Funding options

Examples of recovery projects may include utility upgrades, expanded facilities, and relocation of highways or roads.

Selecting Recovery Projects: Prioritization

Projects that can be accomplished relatively quickly with solid community support and the available financial resources at hand should begin as soon as possible. Completion of these projects will foster and strengthen community support and political endorsement of future projects. The end result of such swift and positive action increases the possibility of a comprehensive recovery effort as the event continues to unfold.

Projects that have the most significant impact to a community-wide recovery should have a high priority. Those projects with the highest recovery value to local residents and community leaders should be pursued and completed as soon as possible.

Public works recovery projects are often at the top of a community's recovery list. Restoration of essential services, repair and reconstruction of critical infrastructure, and provision of services must be accomplished or the community-wide recovery effort may be significantly delayed or come to an unexpected halt.

For example, choosing between two important recovery projects such as the reconstruction of a community center or the hardening of a wastewater treatment facility is a difficult decision because both are important to the community. However, the essential service provided by the wastewater facility makes it a higher priority.

Keep in mind that while pre-defined recovery priorities are critical to the recovery effort, the recovery plan has to remain flexible. It should be considered a guide or framework and may evolve as the recovery process continues.

Lesson Summary

In this lesson, you learned how the recovery plan establishes the basic footprint of the recovery process and the importance of updating the plan when necessary.

The Recovery Task Force plays an important role in the implementation and maintenance of your community's recovery plan.

Remember, the recovery process must be monitored closely, and it is important that results are visible as soon as is possible.

Keep in mind that there will be a number of projects that will need to be completed for the community to recover after a disaster. These should be broken down into short- and long-term projects and prioritized for the community.

When establishing recovery priorities to include in the plan, consider the general prioritization of critical infrastructure and key resources, economic impacts, and the needs of the community.

Lesson 6: Achieving Recovery Goals

Lesson Overview

One of the largest obstacles to any community's or public works agency's disaster recovery plan is the lack of financial resources to implement recovery actions. In this lesson, you will learn about some funding options that may be available after a disaster so you can identify opportunities for achieving recovery goals.

Upon completion of this lesson, you will be able to:

- Differentiate among Individual Assistance, Public Assistance, and other public works related federal programs.
- Explain how public works can use federal disaster assistance programs to advocate for mitigation in the community.
- Describe the benefits of mitigation planning to the community.
- Select recommended mitigation strategies for a community based on disaster information.

Federal Disaster Assistance

When disasters strike, and if certain damage thresholds are met, federal assistance in the recovery process may be available. All major federal disaster assistance programs are derived under the authority of the Robert T. Stafford Disaster Relief and Emergency Assistance Act. Presidential Disaster Declarations are commonly referred to as "Stafford Act" declarations.

The two major disaster recovery programs under the Stafford Act are the Public Assistance Program (PA) and Individual Assistance Program (IA). Additionally, public works entities may have available to them federal funding under non-traditional disaster programs such as Federal Highway Administration (FHWA), Federal Aviation Administration (FAA), or the Bureau of Indian Affairs (BIA).

Stafford Act

As you may recall from the IS-552 course, *The Public Works Role in Emergency Management*, the Robert T. Stafford Disaster Relief and Emergency Assistance Act (Stafford Act) authorizes the President to issue a major disaster declaration to provide federal aid to states or federally recognized tribes overwhelmed by disasters. The Act also defines FEMA's authority to coordinate disaster and emergency assistance to individuals, households, state and local governments, tribes, businesses, and certain nonprofit organizations.

Overall, the Stafford Act:

- Establishes the Presidential Disaster Declaration process

- Defines the relationship among federal, state, local, Native Alaskan village, tribal, and voluntary agencies for disaster efforts
- Authorizes various types of federal assistance from FEMA, depending on the event
- Defines the cost-sharing arrangements between federal, state, local, Native Alaskan village and tribal governments

Public Assistance (PA)

PA is authorized for publicly owned facilities and certain private, nonprofit organizations that provide "like government" services.

The PA program is generally the public works agency's most utilized funding source for recovery.

The PA program will generally reimburse state, local, and tribal governments up to 75% of eligible and documented costs for disaster-related work. The local required portion of PA is 25%, which is often split between state and local governments, in varying percentages.

Keep in mind that this percentage may be different for tribal governments who work directly with FEMA during the recovery process. For example, if the tribe or native village works through a state, it shares 25% of the costs with the state; if working nation-to-nation, the tribe or native village bears responsibility for the full 25%.

The PA program is structured into various categories that provide a recovery framework for public works officials. These categories contain required guidelines for temporary and permanent recovery work including debris management, emergency protective measures, and roads and bridges.

FEMA, the state, and the tribal or local emergency management organization will assist public works officials during the recovery process to ensure compliance with these critical categories. Links to FEMA 322, *Public Assistance Guide*, and FEMA 323, *Public Assistance Applicant Handbook*, are included in the Resource section of the Toolkit.

Individual Assistance (IA)

IA is authorized for individuals and families in a disaster where a state is overwhelmed and a significant number of homes and/or dwellings are damaged or beyond repair. While administrative responsibility for IA does not normally fall under the public works agency's purview, you should be familiar with the program.

Factors that determine an IA declaration include the number of homes impacted, economic ability of the state to respond, special populations within the impacted area, and insurance coverage of the disaster zone(s).

Programs include housing assistance and repair, unemployment compensation, and meeting immediate needs such as assistance for disaster-related medical and dental costs.

FEMA and the local emergency management department are responsible for establishing Disaster Recovery Centers (DRC), where impacted community members can go to register for and receive federal assistance under the IA program and, in some cases, low-interest federal loans from the Small Business Administration (SBA). The SBA remains the largest source of individual and business disaster relief in the United States.

Other Programs

Public works officials often work with projects or partners that can obtain funding outside of the traditional funding streams following a disaster event. It is incumbent upon public works officials to seek such alternate funding when available. For example, if a vital small community airport runway is damaged, public works should seek recovery funding from the FAA before approaching FEMA. Under federal guidelines, FEMA will not repair or replace items (e.g., airport runway) that are under the jurisdiction of another federal agency (FAA).

Additionally, many tribal organizations obtain recovery funding from the federal government that supplements traditional Stafford Act funding. If a project has an existing local government-tribal partnership, or could have such a partnership, then PW can play a critical role in assisting the community with additional funding in the recovery process.

Links to other programs to consult about funding can be found on the Resources page in the Toolkit.

Eligibility for Public Assistance

Certain stipulations apply to projects in order for the costs to be eligible for reimbursement under the Public Assistance program.

General Eligibility

To be eligible for reimbursement under the PA program, costs must:

- Be reasonable and necessary to accomplish eligible work;
- Comply with applicable federal, state, local, and tribal laws and regulations; and
- Include deductions of insurance proceeds, salvage value, and purchase discounts.

Emergency Work Category A: Debris Removal

Examples of eligible work in this category include removal of:

- Trees
- Building wreckage
- Sand, mud, silt, and gravel
- Vehicles
- Other materials

Emergency Work Category B: Emergency Protective Measures

Examples of eligible work in this category include:

- Security forces (police and guards)
- Shelters/emergency care
- Sandbagging
- Bracing/shoring up of damaged structures
- Emergency repairs
- Emergency demolition
- Removal of hazards

Permanent Work Category C: Roads and Bridges

Examples of eligible work in this category include repair of:

- Roads
- Bridges
- Shoulders
- Ditches
- Lighting
- Signs

Permanent Work Category D: Water Control Facilities

Examples of eligible work in this category include repair of irrigation systems, drainage channels, and pumping facilities. There is also limited eligibility for the repair of levees, dams, and flood control channels.

Permanent Work Category E: Buildings and Equipment

Examples of eligible work in this category include repair or replacement of:

- Public buildings
- Content and systems of public buildings
- Heavy equipment
- Vehicles

Permanent Work Category F: Utilities

Examples of eligible work in this category include repair of:

- Water treatment and delivery systems
- Power generation facilities and distribution lines
- Sewage collection and treatment facilities

Permanent Work Category G: Parks, Recreational Facilities, and Other

Examples of eligible work in this category include repair and restoration of:

- Parks
- Playgrounds
- Pools
- Cemeteries
- Beaches
- Work otherwise not covered in categories A-F

Nonprofit Eligibility for Public Assistance

Eligibility of certain nonprofit organizations to receive federal recovery assistance is a relatively new aspect of the PA Program. Examples of eligible applicants, that provide services similar to those provided by governments, may include:

- Dike districts that assist a city by allowing flood waters to be released during an event
- A museum that is a nonprofit
- A private school that provides education much like the public schools within a community
- A Salvation Army distribution center

Many times, the local emergency management agency will rely upon public works to inform them about these types of nonprofit organizations that exist in the community.

Mitigation and the Public Works Official

A major benefit of a Stafford Act disaster declaration is that public works officials have an opportunity to help mitigate the impacts of future disaster events on their respective communities, both in the early and latter stages of recovery. There is a myriad of mitigation programs that public works officials can access in conjunction with emergency management, but the primary opportunities exist within the PA program itself (Section 406 hazard mitigation funding) and with the Hazard Mitigation Grant Program (HMGP) following the disaster event.

Public Assistance Section 406 Mitigation (Section 406)

Commonly referred to as Section 406 Mitigation, this program is considered "on the spot" mitigation while repairing an impacted facility or structure, where it is more practical to mitigate during repairs. For example, instead of merely repairing a bridge that was damaged because a 40-year-old culvert was too small to allow water to pass, using Section 406 mitigation funding, you could repair the impacted bridge while also replacing the culvert to increase its size.

Approval for Section 406 projects comes from the FEMA Public Assistance Liaison assigned to work the disaster event with a local jurisdiction.

Hazard Mitigation Grant Program (HMGP)

HMGP is one of FEMA's Hazard Mitigation Assistance (HMA) grant programs and is the most utilized and effective mitigation program in the United States. The key purpose of HMGP is to ensure that the opportunity to take critical mitigation measures to reduce the risk of loss of life and property from future disasters is not lost during the reconstruction process following a disaster.

HMGP funding is allocated based upon the expected total costs of a disaster event. For most states, the funding will total up to 20% of the total costs of a disaster, offering public works officials a substantial means by which they can advocate for mitigation in areas of the community that repeatedly suffer preventable effects of disasters.

Funding under HMGP can include seismic retrofit of critical public facilities, elevation or flood proofing of publicly owned structures, and even assistance in creating mitigation plans or strategies that may help mitigate disaster events in the future.

After a disaster occurs, mitigation funding under HMGP is usually very structured and requires technical justification of a potential mitigation project; however, each state implements this program in varying ways. Therefore, it is in public works' best interest to research the mechanism that the state has in place before pursuing HMGP funding.

Pre-Disaster Mitigation (PDM) Grant Program

You don't have to wait for a disaster to strike to be eligible for mitigation funding. The Pre-Disaster Mitigation (PDM) Grant Program provides funds to states, territories, counties, Native Alaskan village and tribal governments, communities, and universities for hazard mitigation planning and the implementation of mitigation projects prior to a disaster event.

The PDM program is a nationally competitive program designed to assist states, territories, counties, Native Alaskan village or tribal governments, and local communities to implement a sustained pre-disaster natural hazard mitigation program to reduce overall risk to the population and structures from future hazard events, while also reducing reliance on federal funding from future disasters. PDM grants are awarded on a competitive basis and without reference to state allocations, quotas, or other formula-based allocation of funds.

Public works agencies could use PDM funding for a number of projects, such as seismically retrofitting buildings, hardening critical facilities, or relocating infrastructure.

Additional information on this and other HMA programs can be found on FEMA's HMA website. A link to that website is included on the Resource page in the Toolkit.

Benefits of Mitigation Planning

The mission of hazard mitigation is to reduce the potential impacts from future events or disasters. Evaluation of mitigation opportunities is a part of all aspects of emergency management; further, local governments are required to have a Natural Hazard Mitigation Plan (NHMP).

Identification of mitigation opportunities in the recovery process is crucial to reducing the impact of a future event or disaster. Mitigation planning is similar to recovery planning in that it requires input from all stakeholders, as well as prioritization of efforts and financial resources.

There are significant benefits to including mitigation planning in all parts of public works and emergency management, including recovery. Some of them are:

- Increased public awareness
- Reduced future loss of life and property
- Reduced future needs for response and recovery
- Increased funding eligibility (potentially)
- Reduced business and economic interruption
- Strengthened community partnerships

Mitigation Strategies

It is critical for a community to have a standing mitigation committee or structure at all times, even if informally. A review system for potential projects should be established based on criteria such as the needs of the community, project feasibility, and sustainability. Predetermined policies and procedures will ensure a streamlined method for effectively utilizing mitigation dollars following an event. Mitigation actions are generally categorized as structural or non-structural.

Structural Mitigation Examples

Some examples of structural mitigation actions are:

- Retention ponds
- Berms, levees, and seawalls
- Hardened buildings and essential or critical facilities
- Seismic retrofitting
- Relocation of infrastructure out of a flood zone
- Enlarging undersized culverts

Non-Structural Mitigation Examples

Some examples of non-structural mitigation actions are:

- Building code revision
- Land use management or land acquisition
- Hazard analysis

- Debris management plans
- Mapping and information management
- Local policy development
- Public information and education

Lesson Summary

In this lesson, you learned that the Stafford Act authorizes disaster assistance in many forms, including Individual Assistance, Public Assistance (including Section 406), the Hazard Mitigation Grant Program, and the Pre-Disaster Mitigation Grant Program. In addition, funding from other sources, such as the Federal Highway Administration, may be available for public works mitigation projects.

Remember, the mission of hazard mitigation is to reduce the potential impacts from future events or disasters. Mitigation planning has many benefits for the community as well as the public works agency.

For more information on mitigation planning, download FEMA's series of how-to guides for state and local mitigation planning. These guides are full of helpful information that can help with all aspects of mitigation planning and implementation. A link to these hazard mitigation planning resources is included on the Resource page in the Toolkit.

Course Summary

Public works plays a vital role in helping the community recover from a disaster, and a recovery plan is an essential part of the public works agency's preparedness efforts. Remember that public works recovery planning must coordinate with other agency plans and the community-wide plan.

By completing this course, you should be prepared to implement the steps for developing a recovery plan for your public works agency and for putting the plan into action should it be needed.

www.ingramcontent.com/pod-product-compliance
Lightning Source LLC
Chambersburg PA
CBHW080817280726
48660CB00018B/3488